IMAGES OF

West Wales

Carmarthen Journal

IMAGES OF
West Wales

The Breedon Books
Publishing Company
Derby

First published in Great Britain by
The Breedon Books Publishing Company Limited
Breedon House, 44 Friar Gate, Derby, DE1 1DA.
1999

ISBN 1 85983 151 6

Printed and bound by Butler & Tanner Ltd., Selwood Printing Works,
Caxton Road, Frome, Somerset.

Jackets and colour separations by GreenShires Ltd, Leicester.

Contents

Acknowledgements

This compilation would not have been possible without the help of the many people who readily loaned photographs and postcards depicting west Wales in days gone by. Our thanks go to them and also to those people who provided the information which accompanies the pictures in this collection. Particular thanks go to the following for the loan of photographic material:

John Bessant, Linda Bowen, Carmarthen Museum, Mrs H. Davies, Roger Davies of the Pembroke Collectors' Centre, Mrs S. A. Edgehill, H. B. Enoch, Mrs Eira Evans, Mr Elwyn Evans, E. W. Evans and family, Mr G. Nevyn Evans, Mr David Gealy, Les George, Mec Griffiths, Robin Griffiths, Gordon Howells, David Hughes, Mrs Glenys James, Brian Jenkins, Dan Jones, Mr D. C. Jones, Mr Des Jones, Mrs Julie Jones, Keri Jones, Stuart Ladd, Tony Lee, Mr T. D. Mansfield, National Library of Wales, National Museum of Wales, Pauline Owens, Cyril 'Billyboy' Owens, J. H. Owens, Felicity Pearce, Mrs D. Rees, Mr D. T. Rees, J. M. Rees, Susan Richards, RSU Windows, Coralie Steel, Alan Thomas, Ray Tobias, Donald Williams, Mr P. G. Wright.

Foreword

HERE it is – the book to help you wallow in nostalgia.

The *Carmarthen Journal* is Wales' oldest surviving newspaper – we launched in March 1810 – and during those years we have published thousands of pictures under the banner of 'Down Memory Lane' and, more recently, 'Past Snaps'.

As we approach a new millennium, we thought it a good idea to publish a book of photographs which will record for history some of the more memorable moments of the dying years of this millennium.

I am grateful to our many readers who have responded to our appeal for help in making this book possible. They have loaned us some remarkable pictures from their family albums and the prints tell us a lot about how we were.

I am also grateful to *Journal* journalist Keith Johnson who has spent much time compiling the book. He has examined hundreds of pictures and he was presented with a difficult task in choosing the photographs we have published.

We believe they give a good insight into life in West Wales in the last 120 years.

I trust the book will give you many happy hours of enjoyment.

Alan Osborn
Editor
Carmarthen Journal

West Wales in Camera

How does one begin to define the boundaries of West Wales?

Well, since this collection has been put together by the *Carmarthen Journal*, mainly from old photographs submitted by its readers, our working definition of West Wales is simple – it is the area served by the *Journal*, the oldest weekly newspaper in Wales.

And what a richly varied area this is. There are the coal-mining communities of the Aman and the Gwendraeth valleys, the industrial heritage of which is vividly recalled in numerous photographs in this collection.

There are the sheep-studded hills and there are the two coastlines, the rugged Ceredigion shore with its tiny fishing harbours that have been transformed into holiday resorts, and the Bristol Channel shoreline of cockle-beds and long, sandy beaches.

And, of course, there are the rivers, where the coraclemen still fish for salmon in the time-honoured way, fiercely jealous of their ancient rights.

A rural lifestyle, half-forgotten, is revealed in a fascinating series of pictures of horse-fairs, haymaking and sheep-shearing from the early years of the century.

And there are street scenes aplenty, from market towns and whitewashed villages, in the days before the motor car ruled the world. Indeed, it is difficult, viewing this collection of photographs, not to long for a return to a time when life in West Wales moved at the speed of a horse and cart and you could stand and gossip for hours in the middle of the highway.

But that is looking at the past through rose-tinted spectacles. Life in West Wales has often been difficult in the rural communities and well as the industrial; just look at the work-weary faces of the colliers or the fishermen, the market women, the reapers or the cockle-gatherers whose portraits appear in this collection.

But if the work was hard, there were good times as well to enjoy – acrobats in the park and carnivals in the town square, village fairs, parades and processions, rugby trips and eisteddfod competitions.

And for all these occasions there was a photographer on hand to record the event for posterity, and although they could not have known it, for this collection of *Images of West Wales.*

Old Carmarthen Town

Merlin the wizard's famous prophecy stated: 'When Priory Oak shall tumble down, Then shall fall Carmarthen town.' The oak stood for centuries in Priory Street – alive once, but later a dead and withered fang. Its remains were removed in 1978, but despite the prophecy, Carmarthen is still standing.

The oak may have been a 'Royal Oak', planted to commemorate Charles II's return to the throne in 1660. It was allegedly poisoned in Victorian times by a grumpy townsman who was fed up with noisy groups gathering in the shade and shelter of the tree at all hours of the day and night. As this picture shows, there was little left of the Priory Oak in 1950.

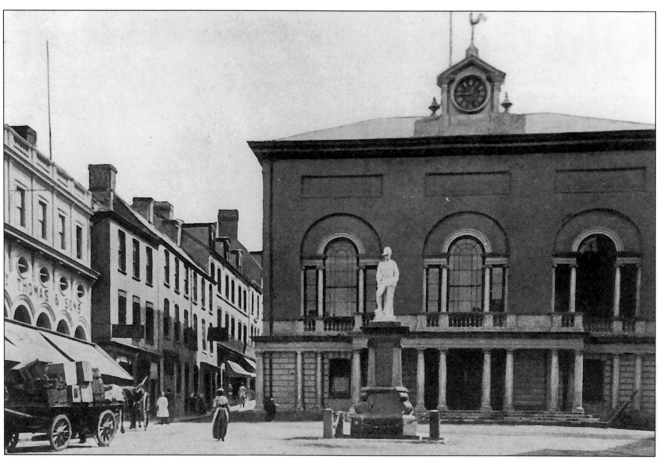

Carmarthen's Guildhall dates from 1767.

The 'coffee pot' sign looms large in this 1930 view of Guildhall Square.

An early motor-bus makes its way past the Angel Hotel in Lammas Street.

Dark Gate, before the attractive buildings on the left were demolished as part of the town centre 'redevelopment'.

The chateau-like county hall, built on the site of the old town jail.

This temporary Bailey bridge across the Tywi helped relieve some of the town's traffic problems in the 1970s.

The Royal Welch Fusiliers monument in Lammas Street, photographed by J. F. Lloyd. The cannon in front of the monument was a trophy of the Crimea War.

A 1960s view westward along Lammas Street.

A lone cyclist pedals into the sunset towards the monument to Sir Thomas Picton.

General Sir Thomas Picton was born in Pembrokeshire in 1758 but lived for much of his life at Iscoed near Ferryside. He served under Wellington during the Peninsular War and again at Waterloo, where he died while leading a cavalry charge apparently while wearing a top hat. This is his monument.

In medieval times, King Street was one of the town's main streets, with the castle at one end and St Peter's Church at the other.

King Street has always been a lively thoroughfare. One resident was the dramatist and essayist Sir Richard Steele who lived there in the early 18th century.

The freedom of the road for this cyclist in Priory Street which takes its name from the Priory of St John the Evangelist.

Priory Street and its youthful inhabitants may look peaceful in this view, but it was not always so. In his marvellous book *The South Wales Squires*, Herbert Vaughan recalled what happened when his family coach had to negotiate Priory Street in the 1880s. "We had to bear the brunt of a running attack made by wild unwashed urchins who pursued the carriage, shrieking, swearing, spitting and throwing mud at it as it passed along the street," he wrote.

Carmarthen's leafy Parade was always a favourite place for a Sunday stroll.

A chauffeur waits patiently outside the Boar's Head Hotel in Lammas Street.

This arcade used to stand in John Street, Carmarthen. At the front was the W. Ben Jones furnishing business, while at the back was Henstock's billiard hall with its ten tables. Above the arcade was the Carmarthen Jubilee Club, and although the whole area has undergone redevelopment in recent years, the Jubilee has managed to remain in much the same spot. The picture probably dates from the early 1950s.

A horse fair outside the Eagle Inn, Priory Street.

An early photograph of Francis Terrace.

Carmarthen market with its attractive clock tower was built in 1846. Happily, the tower was preserved when a new market opened on the same site in 1981.

High Days & Holidays

All the fun of the merry-go-round at Llansteffan Fair.

Brechfa Fair looks to be rather less of a spectacle. The year is 1907.

S. Alberto of King Street, Carmarthen, peddling his wares at Llanddarog Fair.

A procession through Llansteffan to commemorate the coronation of George V.

Residents of the Mwldan district of Cardigan celebrate the coronation of George VI.

Gathering around the wireless to listen to the jubilee broadcast in 1935 are these residents of St Clears.

Regatta time at Carmarthen Quay in about 1950. The coraclemen are William 'Billy' Owens and Steve 'Dwr' Thomas.

A big turn-out of spectators for the annual regatta in Laugharne.

Top cyclists from all over Britain and even Europe would take part in races at Carmarthen Park. This picture was taken at a 1903 bank holiday meeting.

Cycle racing at the Park was still popular in the 1930s.

This picture of acrobats in Carmarthen Park was taken by noted Carmarthen photographer J. F. Lloyd.

Schreyer, 'The Great American Aerial Cyclist', performs his death-defying high dive for the people of Carmarthen. The date is Whit Monday 1905.

A loudspeaker van leads the carnival parade through Laugharne township.

No fears about beef on the bone in those days. An ox roast in the grounds of Laugharne Castle.

A carnival parade passes through Narberth in 1919.

The Village Street

Amroth village in the 1920s.

Pendine Hill.

The post office at Pendine.

Pendine village and hill.

Llanfallteg near Whitland was once a halt on the 'Cardi Bach' railway line.

The village of Clunderwen developed where the railway line crossed the road in the picture – the main Narberth to Cardigan highway.

Another view of Clunderwen. The village was originally called 'Narberth Road' after the railway station which opened in 1854.

Crymych, 'capital of the Preselis'.

The village of Moylgrove near Cardigan.

Pantteg Cross. Note the old style petrol pump.

The post office at Pantteg Cross.

Pont Allt-y-cafan which bridges the Teifi at Pentrecwrt.

A general view of Llandysul.

Lincoln Street, Llandysul.

Llanybydder, with the Railway Hotel in the centre of the picture.

The main road through Pencader.

Fine sea views from Glanmor Terrace, New Quay.

Aberystwyth Road in Aberaeron.

A distant view of Talley with its abbey and lakes.

The lonely village of Cwmdu, north of Llandeilo.

Cilycwm village near Llandovery.

The square in Llangadog.

High Street, Llandybie in 1909.

Station Road, Brynamman.

The height of fashion in Garnant.

The square in Tycroes.

Waterloo Road, Penygroes.

The village street in Bancffosfelen.

Drefach in the Gwendraeth Valley.

Rival chapels dominate this general view of Pontyberem.

The railway line and Furnace Terrace in Pontyberem.

A horse and cart leave the village of Pontantwn.

A view of Porthyrhyd looking westwards, with the Prince of Wales pub on the right.

Porthyrhyd from the other direction.

The southern end of Llanddarog village.

A general view of Llangyndeyrn.

Thatched cottage at Heol y Gwynt, Crwbin.

Pembrey Square with the Commercial Arms on the left.

St Illtyd's Church in Pembrey.

The Ferry Hotel in Ferryside offered 'Burton Ales and Stout on Draught'.

A general view of Llandyfaelog village.

Llansteffan Green.

A view of Llansteffan, looking south.

Conwyl Elfed, north of Carmarthen.

An early motor car attracts attention in Cynwyl Elfed.

The Carmarthen to Lampeter road passes through Alltwalis.

The village street in Llanpumsaint.

Brechfa post office.

Cothi Bridge.

Penrheol, Nantgaredig in 1923.

The Carmarthen to Llandeilo road at Abergwili.

Abergwili viewed from the other direction.

On the Road

Llandovery Town Band travelling in style.

Even in Victorian times, it wasn't always easy to find a parking space in Narberth.

An open carriage and pair leaving Laugharne.

There's even a 'penny-farthing' among this wonderful collection of bicycles outside Carmarthen Guildhall.

Cycling fashions have changed somewhat since these intrepid bikers set off for Alltwalis in 1909.

The first motor car reaches Rhandirmwyn.

Surely the chauffeur is meant to do the driving? This fine vehicle belonged to the Stepney Gulston family of Derwydd, Llandybie.

Evan Morris & Sons, who operated the Big Hat shop in Carmarthen, also delivered clothes to all parts of the county. The Big Hat sign is still on the shop in Lammas Street.

The opening of a regular GWR 'motor-car' service between Carmarthen and Llansteffan in April 1909.

Journey's end – Llansteffan square.

Drivers and porters wait outside Carmarthen station. The Llansteffan 'motor-car' is on the right.

New Quay was also served by a 'motor-car'. This picture is dated 1907.

A charabanc outing to New Quay in 1924.

Motorbiking at Bancffosfelen in the 1930s.

J. James and Sons operated this single-decker bus from the College Street bus depot in Ammanford.

The Laugharne motor bus outside Morgan's Garage.

Jones, Ffoshelig, operated their coaches from this garage near Newchurch, north of Carmarthen.

This picture of the Bwlchnewydd to Carmarthen bus – the 'Newchurch Pride' – was taken in 1922.

Drivers Denzil, Ogwyn, Dai Bach and Iori with their coaches on a Jones, Ffoshelig trip to Porthcawl in 1949.

Heading for the wilds… The bus to Trelech and Mydrim waits for passengers outside the West End Cafe in Lammas Street, Carmarthen, in 1950.

House and Home

Golden Grove near Llandeilo, one of Carmarthenshire's most important country seats. The first mansion was built at Golden Grove in the time of Elizabeth I, but the present house dates from 1826. Along with Stackpole in Pembrokeshire, it was the Welsh home of the Earls Cawdor.

Golden Grove was occupied during the last war by US airmen. In 1952 the mansion and part of the estate were leased to Carmarthenshire county council for use as an agricultural institute.

The 17th century Taliaris house north of Llandeilo was the country seat of the Gwynne family.

Edwinsford, near Talley, showing the bridge built by William Edwards of Pontypridd in 1783. Once the home of the Williams family, Edwinsford is now sadly ruined.

It is reputed that both King John and King Henry VII stayed at Derwydd mansion at various times. The house, beautifully sited near Llandybie, was from the 18th century the home of the Gulston family.

Alltyferin mansion, Llanegwad, was built in 1869 for Swansea businessman Henry James Bath. It remained in the Bath family until 1923, but was demolished soon after the last war.

Amroth Castle an 18th-century mansion with castellated façade, built on the site of a medieval castle.

The Vicarage at Llanddarog was an imposing building.

Walter Vaughan of Cwrt Penbre was High Sheriff in 1557, the manor eventually passing by marriage to the Ashburnham family of Sussex. Although the Lords Ashburnham never lived at Cwrt Penbre, Pembrey Court, it continued to be owned by the family until 1922. The buildings were later used as a farmhouse.

Penllain Cottage, a picturesque thatched dwelling near Pontiets.

Thatched cottages at Grosfaen, Pontyberem.

The delightfully-named Winkin Street, Rhandirmwyn.

Phillips Bach outside his Llandysul home, reputed to be the smallest house in Great Britain. The picture dates from 1935.

Post-war housing at Tyle Teg, Garden Suburb, Burry Port.

Orchard Park estate on the outskirts of Laugharne.

The Maesolbri housing estate in the village of Llanybri.

Rural Life

The local hunt has always been an important feature of rural life. This picture shows a meet of the Carmarthenshire Foxhounds at Pontantwn.

A meet of the hounds at Llansteffan.

Market day in Narberth in 1904. A travelling 'cheap-jack' has laid out his wares on the ground.

Narberth Pig Fair, 1903. Many families fattened a pig each year for bacon.

Country people would flock into town on market day to sell butter, eggs and cheese and perhaps to buy flannel and woollens, clogs and cockles, farm tools and kitchen-ware. This picture shows a typical rural market in Llanybydder.

And while their wives haggled over prices in the market, the farmers would be buying and selling animals at the nearby mart-ground. This is Llanybydder once again.

Sheep have the right of way over Llandeilo bridge in this superb 1910 photograph.

Farmers from the Preseli hills gather at Maenclochog horse fair in 1905.

Cutting the churchyard grass at Penboyr, Felindre, in 1948.

Deiao Ajax, a shepherd whose flocks roamed the hills of the upper Cothi Valley.

The pace of rural life… A cow ambles through the centre of Llanddarog village.

Splitting logs for making clog-soles. Alder wood was favoured by clog-makers, being coarse-grained and soft, and in the spring and summer months gangs of travelling clog-makers would set up temporary camp in the alder groves of west Wales. This picture shows cloggers in action near Llandovery.

Harvesting at Y Fadfa, Talgarreg, Llandysul in 1889. Sickles such as these were gradually being replaced by scythes.

Harvest time at Waun-lluest farm, Llanfynydd, early in the century. Harvesting was always a communal effort, involving men, women and children.

A fine collection of reaping tools in this picture of harvest time at Glan Bran, Cynghordy. The man second from the right has been sharpening the teeth of the mechanical reaper blade using a traditional 'rip'.

Making hay while the sun shines at Bancyfelin.

Time for a break at Bryn Farm, Newchurch, for the Griffiths family…

…And for these harvesters at Waun-lluest, Llanfynydd. A full day's harvesting could run from 5am to 10pm, with a break for a 'siesta' during the heat of the afternoon.

A cartload of hay in the fields above Carmarthen.

Shearing the sheep at Llandyfaelog. On the right is Mr Alfred Morgan of Nantygoetre.

School transport… Children from Lacques Fawr, Llansteffan set off for school by donkey cart. The donkey would find its own way home.

The staff of the village post office at Llanarthne.

There was a time when every village had a shop. This is the grocery and draper's shop in Llandyfaelog.

Llanarthne post office had become part of D. J. Michael's thriving village store by the time this photograph was taken.

On and Off the Rails

A goods train steams across the rail bridge over the Tywi in Carmarthen. The year is 1955.

Carmarthen railway station, looking eastwards. The former road bridge over the Tywi on the left has been replaced by a higher level bridge.

The GWR signalling class at Carmarthen in 1923.

The iron railway bridge over the Tywi was built in 1858. It was demolished in January 1984.

Carmarthen railway staff in the early 1940s. Inspector Gomer Jones is in the front.

Snow on the tracks. The view from The Parade in Carmarthen in the early 1960s.

It was once possible for passengers to travel by train from Burry Port through Pontyberem to Cwmmawr, but this service was withdrawn in 1953. This picture shows the station at Burry Port in the early years of the Gwendraeth Valley Railway.

A train bound for Swansea steams through the GWR station at Pembrey and Burry Port.

Rail-workers watch as a passenger train rumbles past Brigstocke Terrace in Ferryside.

Hard to know what these passengers had to smile about; this was the last train out of Ammanford station before the service to Brynamman was wound up in the 1950s.

A young girl looks across at Llanybydder's attractive little railway station on the Carmarthen to Aberystwyth line.

Bryn Teifi near Maesycrugiau in 1963 a classic branch line station, soon to feel the Beeching axe.

Snow on the line fails to halt operations at a busy Llanpumsaint station in 1911.

Pencader was once a railway junction of some local importance, with a branch line heading off towards Newcastle Emlyn. But the axe fell there too, in September 1965.

Station staff at Pencader in the early years of the century.

A railway gang plus supervisor working on the line somewhere between Pencader and Lampeter.

Food for the fleet. The people of Maesycrugiau do their bit for the war effort in 1914 by dispatching provisions by rail to the Scottish port of Aberdeen.

Cynghordy station near Llandovery was built in the 1860s and remarkably enough is still served by trains travelling between Llanelli and Shrewsbury.

When chapel-goers at Cynghordy raise their eyes to Heaven, they can still see the famous 18-arched railway viaduct carrying the Central Wales line.

People weren't the only passengers on the railways of west Wales. This superb photograph shows horses arriving for the 1904 Dalis Fair – the annual horse fair held in the streets of Lampeter.

The Industrial Landscape

Loading lime for local farms at the kilns in Coygen Quarry near Laugharne.

Coygen Quarry in more recent times.

A traction engine trundles through Laugharne, pulling trucks carrying stone for road repairs.

Carmarthen tinworks flourished in Victorian times, employing a large number of men and women from the eastern end of the town. Its closure in about 1900 was a severe blow to the local economy.

Dafydd Jones of Priory Street, Carmarthen, was the last blacksmith to work at Johnstown forge. He is pictured in about 1950 at the Water Street forge in Carmarthen being closely watched by local youngster David Hughes.

The Cilyrychen lime kilns at Llandybie were built in the 1850s. Designed by R. K. Penson in what was described as Gothic-Moorish-Venetian style, they remain an impressive sight. Penson was primarily a church architect, and in 1871 he modestly described himself as 'architect, landowner, lime burner and water colour painter'.

Snow streaks one of the colliery spoil-heaps at Cross Hands in the early 1960s.

Blacksmith Glan Richard at work in the Water Street forge, Carmarthen. Fourteen men and boys once worked at the forge – welders, machinists, blacksmiths and apprentices. They were employed by Mr William Jones, 'Jones y Lark' of Picton Terrace, Carmarthen.

Capel Ifan Colliery near Pontyberem was a source of stone coal – anthracite. Geological difficulties caused the colliery to close in 1879.

Colliers return from work along the aptly-named Coalbrook Road in Pontyberem.

The pit-head at Cwm Siencyn Colliery, Pontyberem.

Miners and officials of Pentremawr Colliery, Pontyberem.

Ammanford Colliery and Brickworks in the 1920s.

Many of the houses around Llandybie were built with stone from the Pentregwenlais quarry and limeworks.

Blacksmith Elwyn Griffiths who plied his trade at the forge in Cambrian Place, Carmarthen, near the present-day John Street car-park.

Sail and steam vessels take on cargoes of coal in this view of Burry Port docks.

Coast to Coast

Coraclemen on the Tywi in 1882. The traditions of coracle fishing on Welsh rivers go back many centuries and are still kept alive on stretches of the Teifi and Tywi. These Carmarthen coraclemen are (from the left): Thomas William Owen, David Thomas, Willie Owen, Stephen Thomas, Griff Lewis and Harry Evans.

Laurel and Hardy go salmon fishing? Not quite. These are Tywi coraclemen Dai 'Lawdl' Richards and his son Densil of Priory Street. Dai Lawdl weighed 20 stone – a test for any coracle.

A line-up of coraclemen at New Quay regatta in 1949. From the left they are: Ted Blythen, Will Evans, Llew Thomas, Allan Thomas, Lewis Thomas, William Thomas and Steve Thomas, with Ted Price in the foreground.

A Carmarthen coracleman making lines for his net the traditional way, using the longer hairs of cows' tails. These are spun together and wound around a tool known as a 'trwc'. The cows' horns would be sawn into segments to be used as net rings.

Coraclemen on the Tywi. As long ago as 1861, coracle fishermen were described as 'a numerous class, bound together by a strong esprit de corps, who from long and undisturbed enjoyment of their peculiar mode of fishing have come to look on the river almost as their own, and to regard with extreme jealousy any sign or interference with what they consider their rights.'

Joe Elias 'Dan-y-Bancs' was famed for making the most beautiful coracles on the Tywi.

There has always been fierce rivalry between Tywi and Teifi coraclemen. Here Joe Elias strikes a blow for the Tywi boatmen by lifting a coracle above his head to win a competition on the River Teifi in the 1950s.

Keeping the tradition alive. Cyril 'Billyboy' Owens, whose great grandfather appears in the 1882 picture of coraclemen on the Tywi.

William Elias of Carmarthen was Wales' oldest
coracleman when he died in 1973 at the age of 97. He
was still fishing the Tywi well into his eighties and was
awarded the British Empire Medal in 1967 for his role
in keeping alive the art of coracle making and fishing
in Wales.

For many centuries Carmarthen was a thriving port,
and there was a regular coasting trade around the
Bristol Channel and across to Ireland. The 'golden
age' came in the 1840s when the quay was regularly
thronged with sailing schooners and coastal steamers.

The coaster Merthyr outside the corn and flour warehouses of J. B. Arthur on Carmarthen Quay. Vessels carrying flour from Bristol were the last to use the quay on a commercial basis, and this trade ended in 1938.

Burry Port harbour was opened in 1832 as an outlet for the coal being mined in the Gwendraeth Valley.

In 1888 a new west dock was opened at Burry Port to cope with the ever-increasing coal trade. The docks remained in commercial operation until the second world war.

Cockle gatherers on Ferryside sands. In 1925 the villagers of Ferryside landed 29,505 hundredweight of cockles, valued at £4,532.

Donkeys were the traditional means of transporting the haul of cockles to the 'boiling plant'.

Holidaymakers alighting at Llansteffan's North Pier. Llansteffan was a popular destination for day-trippers from the mining valleys, being easily reached via the train to Ferryside and a short boat-ride across the Tywi estuary.

Laugharne was a thriving port in the seventeenth century, with a number of merchants and shipowners living in the township. And since Laugharne was never linked to the rail network, it continued to be served by small coasting vessels into the early decades of this century.

The beach at Pendine has long made it a popular destination for holidaymakers. This photograph shows the village in 1939.

The sea wall at Amroth has taken many a battering from the Atlantic waves.

A coastal steamer negotiates the River Teifi at St Dogmaels. The Teifi Steamship Company continued to operate a number of coastal vessels up until the 1940s, which is when this photograph was taken.

The pier at New Quay was built in 1835, and the small Cardigan Bay port quickly became a centre for shipbuilding. It is said that in the 1840s there were over 300 shipwrights, sail-makers, blacksmiths and rope-makers at work in the village. By the time this photograph was taken, however, New Quay was better known as a popular holiday destination.

Bathing huts line the sands in front of the lifeboat house in New Quay. 'The wild, umbrella'd and french lettered Beach' was how Dylan Thomas saw it in 1944 when he lived nearby.

The village of Llangrannog once owed its entire livelihood to the sea, with virtually all the male population being fishermen, sailors, shipbuilders or sea-traders. The vessel in the picture is a small coasting ketch.

The beach at Llangrannog.

Faces in the Crowd

"Praise the Lord! We are a musical nation." The Emlyn Colliery Brass Band from Penygroes must have made the rafters ring…

…As, no doubt, did the Crwbin Brass Band.

The Felindre Band from the mill villages around Drefach Felindre evidently favoured stringed instruments.

The BBC was on hand to record this 1957 performance by the choir of the Queen Elizabeth Grammar School for Boys in Carmarthen.

Headquarters staff of the 1st Battalion of the Carmarthenshire Home Guard, pictured in 1944.

In their Sunday best for Sunday School – youngsters from Saron near Llandysul.

A branch meeting of the Girls' Friendly Society in Laugharne.

Llangain schoolchildren and their teachers in 1892.

Evans Motors, Carmarthen, was able to field a strong football team in 1947.

Tumble rugby club did the 'double' in 1949-50, winning the West Wales Championship and the President's Cup.

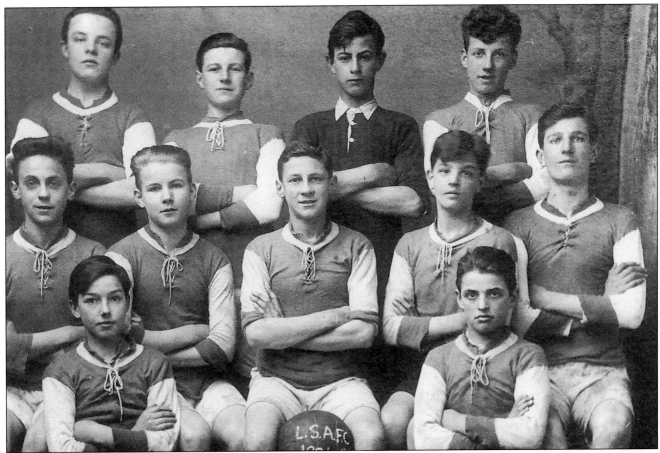

Llandeilo Schoolboys AFC in 1924-25. Second from the right in the middle row is W. Merlin Davies who went on to become a high-ranking churchman in New Zealand.

Carmarthen Wheelers cycling club on their annual outing to the seaside.

Apprentices at Lowndes Garage, Carmarthen.

Competitors in the stockjudging contest at the Carmarthenshire YFC rally at Golden Grove Farm Institute in the late 1950s.

Printing staff at the Carmarthen Journal in the days of 'hot metal'.

Pencader Grammar School pupils enjoy an excursion to Creigau Peb.

A christening picture from about 1900, taken in the studio of Llansteffan photographer D. Griffiths.

St John's Welsh Church choir, Carmarthen, in the 1950s.

The Carmarthen Orpheus glee society. Holding the baton is the conductor Mr P. R. Daniels.

Pontyberem male voice choir which won many prizes under conductor Mr John Williams.

The cricketers of Carmarthen Corinthians in 1948.

Pontyberem cricket club members plus dog.

Llanarthne parish council, 1928-31.

Carmarthen Asylum staff football and hockey club in 1905.

The 'stoolball' team at Drefach school in the Gwendraeth in 1933.

The lawn tennis club at Carmarthen Mental Hospital in the summer of 1922.

Llangunnor school pictured in 1950 when there were just 21 children at the school. In the background is the old Login smithy.

Cross Hands St John Ambulance class in 1906.

Red Letter Days

Princess Elizabeth arrives at Carmarthen to attend the Royal Welsh Show, held near the town in 1947.

The Princess is greeted by Carmarthen Mayor John Jenkins.

By now Queen Elizabeth II, Her Majesty goes walkabout in Lammas Street, Carmarthen.

The Prince of Wales on a flying visit to Pembrey in 1931.

A carefully preserved tradition in Laugharne, said to date back to the 13th century, is the beating of the bounds the Common Walk. This picture and the next three show the Common Walk taking place on a number of different occasions.

The Common Walk is a circuit of about twenty miles around the boundaries of the lordship of Laugharne. The walkers set off at 6am, returning at 6pm "when they go three times round the market house cheering" according to one early account.

The Common Walk takes place every third year on Whit Monday. Those who take part are the burgesses of Laugharne Corporation, usually accompanied by other townspeople and young boys.

The purpose of the Common Walk is to acquaint people with the boundaries of all the land owned by the Corporation. According to Mary Curtis, writing in the 1880s, "The boys are asked if they know the names of the places they come to; if they do not, they stand them upon their heads that it may make them remember the names they tell them."

The Whitsunday Sports at Carmarthen attracted a huge crowd in June 1908, primarily to view the airship flight conducted by the Spencer brothers of London. After an unfortunate mishap when the silk of the balloon was torn and had to be sewn up, the airship finally took to the air at about 7pm.

This was the first-ever airship ascent in Wales, and the successful flight ended near Paxton's Tower at Llanarthne. The airship was inflated with coal gas, and had a 10-foot diameter propeller driven by a 12hp engine.

The induction of the Rev Lloyd Jones at St Luke's, Llanllwni in the 1930s. Seated on the right is Lady Mansel, lady of the manor in Maesycrugiau.

The Gorsedd ceremony at the Carmarthen National Eisteddfod in 1911. In the background is the boys' grammar school.

The Corporation of Laugharne consists of a portreeve, two common attorneys, one recorder, four constables, a bailiff or crier and a foreman of the jury. The portreeve is installed at the Michaelmas Court or Big Court and spends two years in office. This shows the Big Court in 1964.

Traditionally, the first job of the Portreeve is to buy drinks all round at all five of the local pubs.

'The Unveiling and Dedication of the St Clears Memorial Cross erected by the Inhabitants of the Town and District in ever glorious memory of 23 local men who died for their King and Country in the Great War, 19-4 -1918.' The memorial was unveiled in March 1921.

The unveiling ceremony of the Carmarthenshire Boer War Memorial in Guildhall Square, Carmarthen.

On a June day in 1928, the people of Burry Port were surprised to find a Fokker F7 seaplane taxiing into the harbour. The plane had flown from Newfoundland in one of the earliest Atlantic crossings and was bound for London. When the plane ran short of fuel the pilot decided to make an unscheduled landing in the Burry Estuary.

Piloting the seaplane was Wilmur Stulz while the mechanic was Louis Gordon. But most public interest centred on the plane's passenger, Amelia Earhart. She had just become the first woman to cross the Atlantic by air, although in years to come she would gain greater fame by flying solo across the Atlantic and Pacific oceans. She vanished during an attempted round-the-world flight in 1937.

Jim and Amy Mollison at Pendine in July 1933 preparing for an epic 12,000 mile flight from Wales to London via America and Baghdad. The flight ended when their plane *Seafarer* crashed in America, but both escaped unhurt.

Pendine's broad beach has long been famed as a setting for attempts on the world land speed record. One attempt that ended in tragedy came in March 1927 when J. G. Parry Thomas was killed in a high speed crash while driving his car *Babs*. The picture shows the wrecked car being buried in the sand at Pendine, only for *Babs* to be unearthed in 1969 and eventually restored.

This shows a match played at Carmarthen Park for the 'United Kingdom family championship in Rugby football'. On one side were the seven Williams brothers from Haverfordwest, on the other side the seven Randall brothers from Llanelli. The match was played in April 1909, and a scrappy encounter, in which 'a great deal of spleen was imparted', ended in victory for the Haverfordwest family.

Degree day at Lampeter. By tradition, the students would parade through the town from the college to the Town Hall where degrees would be conferred. The *Carmarthen Journal* reported in 1908: "The procession was headed by the pupils of the College School, followed by the graduates and Licentiates (in cap and gown), with the members of St David's College in full academicals."

Supporters salute Plaid Cymru president Gwynfor Evans on winning the Carmarthen seat in Westminster in July 1966 – Plaid's first Member of Parliament.

Youngsters show their support for Carmarthen's new MP.

A Chapter of Disasters

Floodwaters sweep across Pensarn in 1931, recalling the prophecy of the wizard Merlin that one day Carmarthen would be engulfed by floods.

Properties along Carmarthen Quay look to be well under water – a problem they still have to cope with when spring tides coincide with heavy rainfall in the hills.

The swollen river floods Pencader in the unseasonable June of 1935.

Legend has it that when Llandovery flooded in the 1930s, one local character dived out of his kitchen window and swam the length of the main street.

An icy River Tywi flows under the bascule bridge. This railway bridge, built in 1911, was designed to open on a counterweight system to allow ships to reach Carmarthen Quay.

Ice floes drift past Carmarthen Quay during the severe winter of 1962-63.

Harford Square, Lampeter, after the great blizzard of February 1933.

These farmers were on their way to a union meeting in Aberystwyth when their bus left the road near Aberaeron. Only a providential telegraph pole prevented the bus from plunging over the cliff.

The power of the Tywi in full flood can be seen in the following pictures. This photograph shows Dryslwyn bridge near Llandeilo, watched over by the ruined castle.

And this is what the bridge looked like after the floodwaters struck in November 1931.

Another view of the devastated bridge.

Nantgaredig bridge, a few miles downstream, was also damaged but stood up rather better to the force of the river.

Towns and Townships

A 1904 view of Rhosmaen Street, Llandeilo.

Crescent Road, Llandeilo.

The old stables in Ammanford.

Ammanford Square, with the Cross Inn Hotel on the left.

Another view of Ammanford Square.

A cart trundles along High Street, Llandovery in 1912.

Llandovery High Street.

A more recent view of Llandovery Square.

High Street, Lampeter. The Town Hall on the right was erected in 1881.

Bridge Street, Newcastle Emlyn, looking across to Adpar. The date is about 1905.

James' bicycle shop is on the right of this 1911 view of Carmarthen Road, St Clears.

Aptly enough, a lady is travelling along Lady Street, Kidwelly.

Bridge Street, Kidwelly, with the Pelican on the left.

Pinged Hill, Kidwelly.

Rather a gloomy view of Burry Port, with the copperworks stack in the distance.

Station Road in Burry Port. The Railway Hotel is on the left.

Laugharne has always prided itself on being a township, not a village. This is the view from Fern Hill.

A rather dapper cyclist at the entrance to Laugharne.

Newbridge Road, Laugharne.

"So slow and prettily sad…" This view of Victoria Street seems to confirm Dylan Thomas' description of Laugharne in 1939.

People and Places

Was this the first-ever taste of raspberry ripple in Wales? The gentleman on the right is Mr Ben Jones who had emigrated from Carmarthenshire to Pittsburgh, Pennsylvania where he found a job with the Riecks ice-cream company. And when he returned to the old country for a visit in 1939 he brought with him a selection of his firm's ice-cream carefully transported inside freezer compartments on board ship and train. Enjoying a taste of the exotically-flavoured American ices are Mr Jones' sister and brother-in-law Mr and Mrs J. T. Davies and family of Felindre Mill, Dryslwyn.

Sergeant Spurry keeps an eye on the crowd hoping to attend the Greenwood murder trial at Carmarthen in 1920. Harold Greenwood was found not guilty of murdering his wife.

'Mother Jem' outside the Cottage Inn, Lampeter.

Images and works of Dylan Thomas displayed in a Laugharne shop window.

Mr Harold Thomas of Johnstown (left) pictured with brothers Hywel and Mervyn Jones of Cillefwr Farm, Carmarthen. As nephews of the great Jack Anthony who rode three Grand National winners, the brothers were destined to become steeplechase jockeys, and Mervyn rode the 1940 Grand National winner Bogskar. Both brothers joined the RAF early in the war, and sadly both were lost in action.

Three little maids from Pendine.

The thatched New Inn, Ammanford, was demolished in 1910 to make way for the new Lloyds Bank.

Carmarthen had its oak; Llandovery had this magnificent tree in Broad Street.

The West Wales Sanatorium at Llanybydder was opened in 1905 by Princess Christian and her daughter Victoria.

Patients convalesce in the sunshine on the sanatorium terrace.

Newsagent Mr C Snook outside his 'noted picture postcard house' in Burry Port.

The Llansteffan Ivorites Club gathers in force outside the Union Hall Hotel in the village. The Philanthropic Order of True Ivorites was a Friendly Society with a large following in Wales.

Available for concert parties... A Carmarthen Pierrot troupe, photographed by George Weaks of Lammas Street.

Mrs Ada Jones, 'Mamgu Blaenwaun', lived from 1803 to 1888. It was said that she once walked all the way from Llanpumsaint to Carmarthen to watch the last public hanging in the field behind Babell Chapel, Pensarn. Her husband was 'Dafydd y Brenin', a noted 'daughter of Rebecca' who was involved in several raids on toll-gates in the Carmarthen and Pontyberem area.

'Mardy', a tramp who travelled the roads of Carmarthenshire and Cardiganshire in the 1920s and '30s. He was believed to be an ex-miner from the Rhondda.

A Llandovery lady avoids the cobbled streets of the town by keeping to the pavement.

The parish church of St Ishmael near Ferryside with its interesting saddle-back tower. The church was extensively restored in 1860 by R. K. Penson, best known as the architect of Cilyrychen lime-kilns near Llandybie.

A double helping of Baptist chapels at Penybont, Llandysul.

Llandeilo Church.

The beautiful church of Llandyfeisant, Llandeilo.

In the 1940s, one of the oddest attractions around Carmarthen was The Garden of Eden at Glyn Aur, Abergwili, where privet hedges had been trimmed to represent scenes from the Bible. This shows the flight into Egypt.

A topiary version of the Crucifixion.

Nurses and patients take the air at Glangwili Hospital in about 1955.

The horse lines at a Territorial Army camp at Llandovery in 1909.

Church Army mission vans were a regular sight around west Wales in the 1930s.

'Whit Sunday Marchers' gather in Field Street, Ammanford, to listen to the Revd Llwyd Williams.

The cast of *What Happened to Jones* take a photo-call before performing in Carmarthen in 1928.

Crowds gather in Dark Gate, Carmarthen in May 1936 to watch as the *Hindenburg* looms over the town. The German airship was on a flight from America to Germany with 53 passengers, and passed so low over the town that the swastika markings could be seen quite clearly. The *Hindenburg* was destroyed in an accident the following year.

Kidwelly's Norman castle with St Mary's Church in the background. The church was once part of a Benedictine priory.

Llandovery College in the 1920s. The college was founded in 1847 when it promised 'a good, sound classical and liberal education fitting for young men destined for any liberal or scientific pursuit to be exercised and followed in the Principality of Wales'. These days the college is best known as a breeding ground for Welsh rugby internationals.

The Amman Hotel at Glanamman.

The Ashburnham Hotel at Pembrey.

Carmarthen Quins rugby supporters in good voice.

Mr Thomas outside the store that bore his name in Burry Port.

Running repairs to the Town Hall clock in Laugharne.

A more recent view of the Town Hall.

Llanddarog schoolchildren on their best behaviour in 1906.

The end of the Great War is celebrated in the window of Elias and Emmanuel's shop in Quay Street, Ammanford.

Pencader war memorial with a train chugging past in the background.

Later Days

The Western Counties Agricultural Co-operative Association on the Pothouse Wharf – a relic of the days when animal feed was still arriving at Carmarthen by ship.

A sorry-looking WCA building shortly before demolition.

The National Eisteddfod was held in Carmarthen Park in 1973. This picture shows the Gorsedd stones being erected.

Nelson stands alone. The Nelson Hotel in Red Street, Carmarthen survived the first wave of town centre demolition, only to perish in February 1973 as the redevelopment swept all before it.

The area around Carmarthen market before the new market building was erected in 1981.

The market clock tower came through the changes unscathed.

Some things never change. The Carmarthenshire Hunt at a meet in Laugharne in the 1960s.

Pendine has continued to attract daredevils in pursuit of land speed records. Barry Bowles' 1978 attempt ended spectacularly with a puncture at 280mph. He walked away unscathed from the smash.

Pentrepoeth School, Carmarthen: Built in 1897 in solid red brick. Demolished in 1990 to create yet more car parking space. Former pupils include Norman Lewis, widely regarded as Britain's greatest living travel writer.

Carmarthen's John Street in the 1970s.

Compare this fairly recent view of King Street, Carmarthen, with the picture on page 16 in this collection.

And we finish as we began, with the Priory Oak, shortly before its petrified remains were finally removed from the spot where it had stood for 300 years.